Rise and Shine Anytime

Simple Questions To Wake Up Your Life

**Written and Illustrated by
Anne Barry Jolles**

Jolles Publishing

This is not a therapeutic technique for a traumatic event that needs healing or an overwhelming emotion that needs to be more deeply explored or expressed in a therapeutic environment.

Jolles Publishing
72 Damon Road
Hanover, MA 02339
Phone: 781.878.8589

"Rise and Shine Anytime"
Simple Questions To Wake Up Your Life

ISBN: 978-0-9765741-5-6
Library of Congress Control Number: 2008900354

First Edition: July 2005
"G.R.A.C.E.
5 Steps For Bringing Your Best To The Next Moment"

For more information:
Website: www.annejolles.com
Email: abjcoach@comcast.net
Phone: 781.878.8589

Edited by Marilyn Schwader of Clarity of Vision and Virginia Maness

Cover Design and Illustrations by Anne Barry Jolles
Graphic Design by Mandie Wendel and Rana Graphics

For my husband Jon
and my children,
Rob and Alexa

Preface

"Rise and Shine Anytime" was created at a tough time in my life. With so much happening at once, I found it hard to actually engage in my life and move forward. Sound familiar?

I craved a way to step out of the chaos and into calm and found myself saying, "I need to step into grace". Then somehow, it happened. I saw five words within GRACE that encouraged me to ask the questions within those words... and amazing things began to unfold. Though my life and work situations weighed heavily upon me, these questions allowed me to move through them and to invite and create opportunities for what I desired to show up. Since then, this simple process has been my companion through good times and bad.

I have shared it with thousands of others who are incorporating this wisdom into their lives- cancer survivors, entrepreneurs, people in recovery, parents, caretakers, teens, therapists, executives, teachers, doctors, coaches and ministers...

GRACE reminders are hanging on refrigerators, bulletin boards, computer screens, and cubicle walls. They act as prompts to ask the simple questions that lead to amazing results.

In our fast-paced lives, it is essential to access our inner wisdom and to make choices that focus on and nurture what matters most. The GRACE questions are a simple way to open our minds and our hearts to what is possible within each moment. These simple steps provide a doorway to insight and a step beyond what we already know.

I have tried unsuccessfully to find a definition of GRACE that would speak to all. What I do know is what it feels like when it shows up... and it does show up. Part of the challenge is noticing it. GRACE happens *and* these questions help to create the circumstances that actually invite and attract it..

Funny thing about life... it keeps going whether you are ready or not. You will now be able to find your energy and vitality buried among your life challenges. This book is like having a secret recipe in your pocket that can be pulled out when you wish to tap into life more fully and access the unlimited possibilities available to you...

With Gratitude,

Anne

Everyday you choose
to ground yourself
in sanity or
insanity.

The difference is a little grace.

Let this book be the space for you
to ask the questions,
make the choices and
and before you know it,
live the answers...

What's In It For You?

- Increase opportunities for joy in your life.
- Create and savor situations that increase your life satisfaction.

- Clarify those things that keep you stuck.
  - Stop being dragged by life and choose your next move.

- Become a good observer of what is going on inside of you.
  - Separate what is in your control and what is out of your control.

- Regain your footing following a challenge.
- Be proactive and challenge yourself to move closer to where you want to be.
  - Ask for what you want.
  - State your intentions.
- Use your imagination to envision your future.

- Step into a more expansive perspective where much more is possible.
- Tap into your inner knowledge and intuition, discover your own answers and create your future.

How to Use This Book

Open this book to any page,
ask a question and answer it.

OR...

Take the 5 simple steps:
Open this book to any page
in the G section,
ask and answer one Gratitude
question.
Proceed through each letter in
GRACE,
choosing one page in each section,
asking and answering a question,
through the letter E for Embrace.

GRACE

11

is for

GRATITUDE

Beliefs About Gratitude

Appreciation of what is
going right in your life can lead to
increased contentment and satisfaction.

Savoring of good events in your past
contributes to an elevated
feeling of happiness.

Sharing your gratitude with others enhances
your positive feelings and
your relationship with them.

Gratitude will elevate you above the small
details of your life.

Operating from a perspective of gratitude
can increase overall life satisfaction,
which may positively
change your perspective.

Acknowledgement of what you appreciate
in just this moment or in this day
will bring you into the present moment.

Anticipation of events in the future
that make you feel gratitude and joy
will elevate your level of positive feelings.

Gratitude brings you into the present
moment.
Joy lives in the present moment.
Training yourself to stay in the here and now
will increase opportunities
for joy to enter your life.

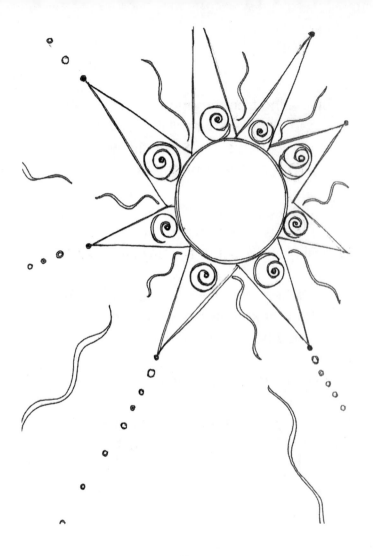

A Metaphor for Gratitude

The sun shines warmly
upon the earth,
bringing us light and energy.
It shines through all seasons
and is necessary as
an energy source to all living things.

What can I do to invite light
and warmth into my life?

G

What is going right
in my life?

How can I make
more of that happen?

"When I try to recall that
long ago first day of school,
only one memory
shines through:
my father holding my hand."
~ Marcelene Cox

Can I recall a time when
I felt cherished?

How can I do that
for another?

Remember a time when a life
situation wasn't working
and I overcame "it".

What is the gift hidden there
that I am grateful for?

How can I use that gift
today?

If I were to send a card
expressing my appreciation
to someone in my life,
to whom would the card
be addressed?

What would it say?

When I _____,
I feel most satisfied and
connected
in a meaningful way.

What am I doing
at those times?

What am I connected to that
makes me feel that way?

I remember a happy time
when I was a child...
I used to love to

_____.

What did that feel like?

How can I invite
more of that into my life?

Think of a time in my life
when I felt
my inner strength...

What was happening?

How did that feel?

I want to tell a story about the best times I have had

_____.

In looking at the whole experience,
what made me feel alive?

What am I grateful for?

Pick one and
give details for the answer:

What delights me?

What makes me
laugh out loud?

Gratitude is like a
spotlight shining on
what is going right in my life.

Where do I want
to shine that light?

Can I remember a time when
my true worth felt honored?

By whom?

How did that feel?

What are 3 things that I value about myself ?

1._____
2._____
3._____

How are they gifts to others?

When I consciously and
deliberately slow down and
pleasantly lose myself
in the moment...

What do I gain?

What am I grateful for?

I will search for and
find something that is
going right in my life.

I breathe in gratitude.

How can I make this a habit?

_____

makes my life worth living.

How can I get more of that?

I think of something or
someone that
I really appreciate...

And say 'hello' to the
energy of gratitude.

How can I encourage
that energy to grow?

How can I share
this energy?

G

When I think back over the
past 24 hours,
what are 3 things that
I am grateful for?

1._____
2._____
3._____

What if I end everyday
with this as my last thought
before sleep?

What can I appreciate right now?

...right here?

...in just this moment?

Who in my past has made a
positive impact on me
and my life?

If they were standing in front
of me,
what would I say?

What am I grateful for?

How can
I open my heart for more?

How would that feel?

What is something that I
have done that
I wish I could be
congratulated for?

What can I say to me?

_____

_____

_____.

I value _____
   so much that
if it was taken from me,
I would lose my breath.

How can I honor today
   what I so value?

What will that look like?

<u>A Way To Connect With</u>
<u>More Joy</u>

Stop

Breathe

Look around

Ask,
"What am I grateful for?"
Do this 3 times a day.

What experience have I
recently enjoyed?

How can I savor it?

How can I share this
with others?

I think of a time when
I felt happy or joyful...

What image comes
to my mind?

I will cherish the feeling
of joy in my heart.

How can I remind myself of
that image daily?

Where in my life have I had
to tap into my honesty
in order to face a challenge?

How am I stronger?

What about that
experience has
made me grateful?

There is always pressure to
do more
and to do it faster.

Within my busy day,
how can I deliberately and
consciously
focus on one pleasurable
situation?

How can I make that
happen more frequently?

What is one moment that
I am proud of?

What about that moment
shows me at my best?

How can I savor that?

How can I express
gratitude to myself
on a daily basis?

What would that include?

How would that sound?

How can I make this
happen?

"Gratitude makes sense of
our past,
brings peace for today
and creates a vision
for tomorrow."
~ Melody Beattie

What is true about that
for me?

What moment can I recall
where I felt wonderfully
connected to
what is most important to
me?

What is it
about that moment that
I am grateful for?

How can I hold on
to that feeling?

What is a moment
that required me to be
courageous,
and I was?

How did I show
courage?

How does that moment make
me feel grateful?

"Only with the heart can a person see rightly,
what is essential is invisible to the eye."
~ Antoine De Saint-Exupery

I put my hand over my heart and ask...

"What does my heart see that makes it feel warmth?"

What is going right in my life?

...in my home?

...in my work?

...in my play?

Life moves so fast.

Today, I will pay attention to
the details of ordinary life.

Where can I find
gratitude in the ordinary?

So many hours are spent
thinking about
the things I don't have.

What things,
already within my grasp,
am I grateful for?

Joy lives only in the present.

What "Aha!" is hidden in that statement for me?

What brings joy to me?

What joy do
I bring to others?

What is the
most important thing that
I have contributed in my life?

What is the gift?

Who in my life supports and
believes in me?

How can I
show them my gratitude?

What gifts have
they given me?

I think of all that
I am grateful for.

I breathe it in.

How can I pass it forward?

What connections
am I grateful for?

How can I let them know?

How can I
make them stronger?

What, for me,
is the sound of gratitude?

How can I hear that
more often?

I need to say, "Thank you".

Whom or what must I thank?

How do I do that?

"Feelings of gratitude
release positive endorphins
throughout the body,
creating health."
~ Sharon Huffman

How can I create
these feelings?

"The more light you allow
within you,
the brighter the world
you live in will be."
~ Shakti Gawain

How can I invite light
to shine in my shadows?

"The deepest craving of
human nature is
the need to be appreciated."
~ William James

Where does this show up
in my life?

How can I express
appreciation to others on a
daily basis?

What 5 things am I grateful for?

1. _____
2. _____
3. _____
4. _____
5. _____

Relationships are like bank
accounts...
It all depends what you put
into them.

What is in my
bank account of good will?

How can I make a deposit
into this account?

A recipe for stepping into the present moment:

Stop...

Notice...

Breathe...

Appreciate...

What showed up?

Think of someone or
something
that I appreciate...

Without words,
I will find the place in my
body where gratitude and
appreciation reside.

What energy flows
from that place?

is for

Release

Beliefs About Release
and Letting Go

You must clarify what it is you want and
need to release before you can let it go.
This is not always easy.

Holding on to people or events that prevent
you from moving forward can block
your view and taint your perspective.

We often try to avoid
the discomfort around letting go
by denying, distracting and blaming others.

When you clarify what is holding you back in
this moment,
you can then choose
what you want to do about it,
whether that is continuing to hold on,
placing it down for a while, letting go of parts
or all of it.

Letting go in one area of your life
can bring freedom into other areas
as you access more energy.

Fear and self-doubt often appear when
you let go or consider letting go.
It may appear easier to
stay in discomfort or pain
rather than to step into the unknown.

Releasing may take hard work, courage,
sweat and honesty.

A Metaphor for Release

It is a sunny, cool autumn day in
New England.
Nature is in all of its brilliant glory
as vibrantly colored leaves
fall from the trees.
This release is a necessary part of
the preparation for winter.
The falling leaves clear the way for
new growth in the spring.

What do I need to release to
prepare for my next season?

I am trying to control

_____.

I cannot control

_____.

What is the big "Aha!" that I
need to grasp here?

"There is a time for departure
even when there's
no certain place to go."
~Tennessee Williams

Where is that true for me?

How does being
judgmental of others
hold me back?

How is my judgment about
others really about myself?

How could releasing this
judgment free me?

Worry steals
my present moments and
my peace of mind.

Is it something
I have control over?

What price do I pay
for worrying?

What can I let go of?

How does the battle between
keeping the peace and
speaking the truth
show up in my life?

What would happen if
I let go of the need for peace
when truth is called for?

I have had it!

I am so sick of

_____!

Now, what can I let go of?

What keeps me from
doing what I know I need
to care for myself?

What can I push out of the
way to move
in that direction?

"The key to change...
is to let go of fear."
~ Roseanne Cash

Who holds that key?

STOP!

I ask my heart and
my soul,

"What must
I let go of today?"

And now, listen...

My intuition is my ally...

Where should I be listening
to my intuition
instead of fighting it?

If I could stop fighting it,
what would I hear?

Something feels unfinished.

What is it?

What do I need to let go of
in order to finish it?

I feel like I am carrying a fifty pound boulder that is so heavy, it weighs me down. When carrying this boulder, I do not have a free hand.

This boulder represents

_____.

Who does it belong to?

What are my choices?

Is there some yearning in me
that struggles to be free?

What wall can I break down
to set it free?

Something just doesn't
feel right...

What adjustments
do I need to make?

What can I release?

What part of my body
feels tight or stiff?

What am I doing when this
occurs?

What emotion is stuck there?

How can I release it?

How can I write the
last chapter
when I am still
working on the middle
of the book?
of the book?

What can I surrender?

When I think about the
challenging situation of

_____,

what outcome am I trying
to control?

How can I release my grip
around controlling
the result?

"Sometimes we all have to
do things
we don't want to do...
even if they seem strange
and scary at first."

~ Unknown

How is this true in my life?

What needs to be let go?

At times,
my voice is so quiet.

Who needs to hear me
speak loudly and clearly?

If no one could hear me,
what would I yell?!

When I think that I am not
good enough,
smart enough,
attractive enough...

What can I let go of so my
"enough" is enough?

If I had a big broom with
which to make a
clean sweep of my brain,
what would I sweep out?

How about my heart?

I cannot save anyone else.

They have to find their
own way.

Where do I draw the line?

I will recall a time when
I felt humiliation
at the hands of another.

If I were to re-create the
situation in my mind,
how would I change it?

Can I imagine and visualize
a different outcome?

What can I let go of?

I feel as though
I have bound my hope
into a package that
must look a certain way.
I hope

_____.

What if I give myself
permission for this package
to look different and
still be okay?

How is this about letting go?

_____and_____
and_____ really
scare me.

What is the probability that
each of these things will
actually happen?

How can I release my worry?

In my life,

_____

plugs into my fears.

How can I unplug this
person or situation?

What would that release?

When and where has my
garden stopped blooming?

What weeds need
to be pulled?

What "Aha!" is buried there?

If I could let go of my fears
and say something that
would make a difference...
and everyone
could hear me...

What would I say?

If I let go of caring about the
judgment of others,
what would I take more of
in my life?

I visualize a big, old
padlock connected to a
heavy, rusty chain encircling
my ankle. The links are cold,
rough and tight.
I cannot walk far.

What or who is represented
by that lock and chain?

How can I release myself
from it?

What are 5 factors that make it difficult for me to reach my objective?

1._____
2._____
3._____
4._____
5._____

How can I release the excuses?

"I should…"

What big "I should" is
driving my thoughts today?

What if I replace "should"
with "want" or "need"?

I "want"_____.

or

I "need"_____.

If I could let go of analyzing
and reporting the facts
of my everyday life,
what would be
hiding behind that?

What lies do I tell myself?

Am I ready to
tell myself the truth?

What will this
truth release in me?

Two rules of the Universe:

Change is inevitable.
Everyone resists change.

What is changing?

What am I resisting?

"In the beginner's mind
are many possibilities:
in the expert's mind
there are few."
~ Susuki Roshi, Zen master

Where can I let go of
being an expert?

What question might
a beginner ask?

What story do I hold onto
because
it hides how I really feel?

Is it time for a
new, updated version?

How can
I let go of the old story?

I will put away my "to do" list
and let go of those items
for now.

I will be silent and
breathe deeply and
ask myself,

"What is on the 'to do' list
of my heart?"

How is impatience an
impediment to my
moving forward?

How would patience impact
my moving forward?

What needs to be let go?

The Serenity Prayer

"God, grant me the serenity
to accept the things
I cannot change,
courage to change the
things I can, and
wisdom to know the
difference."

~ Reinhold Niebuhr

Where am I wasting my
energy on something I
cannot change?

"The world is round and
the place which may seem
like the end
may also be the beginning."
~ Ivy Baker Priest

What would change if
I let go of
there needing to be
a beginning *and* an end?

"Where in my life have
I been a victim?"

How is that
showing up in my life?

How can I let go of that?

Who can help me?

I am working hard
on a dream.

Whose dream is it?

What part of the dream isn't
working and
needs to be released?

Am I so attached to the
outcome that I have
stopped seeing what is
right in front of me?

How can I let go of
what is blocking my vision?

I am struggling with

_____.

How am I taking
this struggle personally?

What is it time to let go of?

How is a concern for
"looking good"
driving my decisions?

What is true?

What do I need to let go of?

If I could let go of my fear,
what changes would
I make in my life?

What would I do?

Where would I go?

I have the right to
change my mind.

Where do I want to do this?

Where do I need to do this?

"There's only one corner of
the universe you can be
certain of improving,
and that's your own self."
~ Aldous Huxley

What improvement am
I resisting?

What needs to happen?

I will become very quiet...
and take a deep breath
and ask...

"Where is emotion
stuck in my body?"

What am I feeling in there?

How can I release the
energy of this emotion so
that it is free to leave
my body?

There is a negative voice in
my head that
nags me and
holds me back...

What is it saying?

What can I say that is true
to quiet that voice?

When looking at my biggest challenge, I will cut "why" out of my vocabulary and...

I will instead begin questions with "what" or "how".

What is a question that needs to be asked that begins with "what"?

...and "how"?

is for

ACKNOWLEDGE

and

ACCEPT

Beliefs about Accept and Acknowledge

To acknowledge is to
see and hear others.

To be acknowledged is to be
seen and heard by others.

To acknowledge is to see *it* and
feel *it* clearly, "It is what it is..."

To acknowledge another's feelings or
the impact of their actions on you produces
a very strong effect in your relationship.

Acceptance is captured in the saying,
"I consider the possibility
that everything
is happening as it is meant to."

Once you accept,
serenity and peace are possibilities.

Acceptance follows acknowledgment.

You can acknowledge and not accept,
though you cannot accept
without acknowledgment.

To accept what you can't control allows you
to stop fighting battles that you cannot win.
Acceptance breeds choice and
is not the same as giving up,
feeling defeated or becoming a victim.

Compassion, courage and honesty
may be necessary.

There is wisdom in emotion.
Acknowledging and accepting
your emotions,
instead of denying, avoiding or blaming,
can open you up to your inner wisdom.

Acknowledgment and acceptance require an
inner quiet as you observe what is going on
not only around you but also within you.

A Metaphor for
Accept and Acknowledge:

It is a cold, crisp winter day,
just after a storm.
The snow is drifting and piled high.
It is quiet, peaceful and everyone
is inside, snug and warm.

I pause, looking around.
There's plenty of time to take it all
in. It is just right for observation,
introspection and reflection.

When I sit quietly,
what emotion do I feel?

131

I am at my best when I

_____

and

_____.

How can I do more of that?

"You are the only one who knows what's happening in your heart and mind. You are the only one who hears your internal conversation - who knows when to withdraw or feel inspired."

~ Pema Chodron

Shhhh!
What do I hear now from inside myself?

"Listening is a form of accepting."
~ Stella Merrill Mann

What keeps me from listening?

What significant event
happened today?

How do I feel about that?

When do I feel the most
understood, listened to
and heard?

How can I do this
for another?

The area most lacking
in my life is

_____.

My hope is that

_____.

The image that captures
that hope is

_____.

How am I honoring my
health and vitality?

Where in my life
am I moving faster than
my guardian angel can fly?

What is at stake?

I get the knowledge, guidance and support that I need when I connect with

_____.

How can I connect more often?

"You never find yourself until
you face the truth."
~ Pearl Bailey

When I turn and
look inward...

What truth do I see?

In looking at my life,
where is
more honesty called for?

What about that scares me?

What is not acceptable?

The two people I most
admire are _____
and _____.

I admire them for their

_____.

What would they
encourage me to accept?

Acknowledgement is not
bragging...

My biggest strengths are

_____

and

_____.

How can I acknowledge them
so they show up more often?

My intuition can supply me
with what I need to know...

What am I ready to ask for?

What am I willing to accept?

"The willingness to accept responsibility for one's own life is the source from which self respect springs."
~ Joan Didion

What responsibility am I willing to accept?

I want to recognize that
nothing is more important
to me than

_____.

How can I acknowledge this
everyday in my life?

If I could stop fighting *it*,
avoiding *it* or denying *it*,
then...

What would I be able to
acknowledge?

My peace of mind and vitality
are being stolen by:

_____

and

_____.

What permission
is being granted?

By whom?

What is sitting
right in front of me and
I refuse to look at it or
talk about it?

With whom do
I need to set boundaries?

What do these boundaries
look like?

...sound like?

...feel like?

"A man should never be
ashamed to own
he has been in the wrong...
in other words,
that he is wiser today than
he was yesterday."
~ Jonathan Swift

Where is the wisdom in
my last mistake?

Which would I compare
myself to:

an old, used tennis ball
or
a new, bouncy super ball?

How high do I bounce?

I will sit quietly and
still my thoughts as
I continually
drift back toward calm.

I will breathe in that quiet.

Now I ask,
"What is right in front me?"

What is calling out to be
seen and heard?

Where do I intend to be
in two years?

What about in five years?

There is wisdom in emotions.

What emotion do
I need to acknowledge
in order to
receive the wisdom from it?

"A fool is someone whose pencil wears out before his eraser does."

~ Marilyn vos Savant

How does this speak about my pencil?

...my life?

_____ just ain't working.

I want to acknowledge

_____.

I will try to accept

_____.

What is the next step?

_____

has worked so hard at

_____.

I want to recognize that and
acknowledge that.

How can that happen?

Sometimes acknowlegdment
is so much easier than
acceptance.

I acknowledge_____
and_____
                    and
I cannot accept_____
and_____.

Three challenges I have
faced and overcome are:

1._____
2._____
3._____

How was I creative?

How was I resourceful?

Sometimes,
when things come too easily,
I take them for granted.

What things am I taking for
granted right now?

Do I believe what I see
or
see what I believe?

Each morning,
what motivates me to
swing my feet out of bed and
put them on the floor?

What are ten reasons that
make my life worth living?

I have a dream that
was interrupted.

How am I feeling about that?

What can I not accept
about that?

Where do I run for cover
when I get uncomfortable?

Official Comfort Zone List:

_____

_____

_____

_____

How does this serve me?

How does it hurt me?

"Inch by inch,
life's a cinch.
Yard by yard,
life is hard."

~ Unknown

What needs to be
acknowledged
in this inch of my life?

What is really hard?

Living life is
like steering a ship;
one has to begin turning
miles before the intended
destination.

Where is my
ship headed?

In what direction do I need to
begin to steer in order to get
me where I need to be?

How are my childhood experiences coloring my reactions to things?

What needs to be said?

To whom?

How do
accomplishments and
success drive me?

How can I acknowledge
myself for who I am, as well
as for what I accomplish?

What about others?

If I let myself feel anger,
what am I angry about?

Where does that
anger live inside me?

How does it affect
me physically?

I will make a wish list
(and not judge it)
that includes the
possible, unlikely AND silly.

Official Wish List

_____

_____

_____

_____

What do I believe I deserve?

When I can silence
my inner voice of criticism,
what do I know to be true,
strong and good about
myself?

I am_____.

I am _____.

I am _____.

I am so afraid that I
will fail at_____.

I know that I cannot control
the outcome of_____.

There is a lesson here...
an "Aha!".

What do I need to learn?

How is this
an opportunity for me?

_____

"downloads" their frustration
and anger to me.

How am I allowing this?

Whose problem is it?

Today's Official Worries:

_____

_____

_____

_____

What things can I *actually*
change or influence?

What needs to be accepted?

When I think about doing
something differently,
I hear_____

When I think about doing
something differently,
I feel_____

Are these thoughts and
feelings the truth?

What is the truth?

I think of the decision
I have to make...

My head says

_____.

My heart says

_____.

My soul says

_____.

"I'm tired, is it much farther?"

When am I saying this
to myself?

About what?

How long have I
been saying this?

Where do I experience the most self-doubt?

What is it that I need to acknowledge in order to quiet those doubts?

How can I remember that?

When I am around _____,
I feel distracted, small
and unnecessary.

How can I acknowledge and
focus on my strengths?

What one image of me
at my best
would I like to
hold in my heart?

Where can I hang this image
so I can see it frequently and
remind myself?

What is the universe
trying to tell me?

What is the universe
ready to offer me?

What am I willing to accept?

If I had a magic wand,
I would create more

_____

in my life.

And I would make

_____

go away.

What about these things do I
need to accept?

Sometimes, it helps to look at
the parts of myself that
I may not like.

When have I been
_____ in the past?

How is it showing up today?

is for

CREATE
and
CHALLENGE

Beliefs About Create
and Challenge

Challenge and creation
are full of action.

Choosing to create something and
stating that intention aloud or
committing it to paper,
will make it more likely to happen.

Inspiration, enthusiasm,
creativity and energy,
as well as necessity and desperation,
can be the sparks
that ignite and spur you into action.

Consciously challenging yourself will
move you closer to
where you want and need to be.

A challenge may be something given to
someone else.

Visually imagining what you wish to create
and choosing your next steps from there,
will carry you closer to that vision.

Challenge and creation do not have to be
tangible. They can be about attitude or
the space you need and desire in your life.

Self judgment, criticism, fear of failure and
humiliation crush creativity.

Honesty, courage and curiosity live
within challenge and creation.

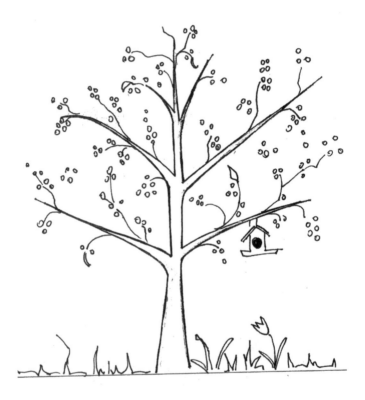

A Metaphor for Create and Challenge

It's spring and the days are
getting longer, lighter and warmer.
The sun is waking up the earth.
The vibrant energy of
inspiration, enthusiasm and
creativity are everywhere.
The once dormant garden is now
alive with green sprouts
poking through the moist soil, and
buds appear on the trees.

What do I want to plant in my life?

There is a knock on my door
and I hear...

"Can *you* come out
and play?"

What do I want
to be invited to do?

How can I create that in my
life?

"An idea not coupled with action will never get any bigger than the brain cell it occupied."
~ Arnold Glasgow

What idea
am I ready to move on?

How?

I will be clear when I ask for what I want and need.

I am going to ask for_____.

How can I do this daily?

What would that look like?

How am I allowing the words
"I'm sorry" to be an excuse
for doing nothing?

What action do I
want to take?

What action am I going to
ask of others?

"Don't let the good things
in life rob you of
the best things."
~ Maltie D. Babcock

Where am I settling?

How can I strive for the best?

How can I treat myself as
well as I treat others?

What will that look like?

How can I challenge myself?

What commitment
will I make?

C

Where am I saying "yes"
when I know in my heart I
should be saying "no"?

My challenge is:

_____.

What do I need to
push out of my way?

In one year I will
be_____

In five years I will
be_____

What 10 minute a day
commitment am I willing to
make to get me there?

How does my "to do"
list cut me off from others?

And myself?

What is my challenge?

Where are my choices
taking me in my life?

What are two changes
I could make to take me
where I want
and need to go?

As the world becomes more
and more cyber-connected,
we lose our real connections
to each other.

How can I
build and strengthen
meaningful relationships?

What do I have to do
differently?

Where can I focus my attention that would lead to a big "Ta-Da!" today?

How about a little one?

If I were to start treating

_____

as though he/she were creative and resourceful, how would that change our relationship?

What would that look like?

If I look at the big picture,
what is my
most important challenge?

Where am I focusing
my energy and attention?

Where am I saying yes when
I need to be saying no?

What challenge am I
facing that
only my heart can unlock?

Is there a challenge
I would like to give to
someone else in my life?

How can I deliver it for
the most desired impact?

I will write an unedited,
no-criticism-allowed,
outrageous story about
something I wish to do.

"I am going to _____
and _____
and then _____.
_____ will show up to join
me as my ally."

What now?

What if today, all day,
I approached each challenge
with humor?

What would that create for
me?

...for others?

It's said that you can't
catch a fish
unless you put your line
in the water.

How can I challenge
myself to put my line
in the water?

"The most powerful agent of growth and transformation is something much more basic than any technique: a change of heart."
~ John Welwood

Where is a change of heart necessary to move forward?

How does that help with my next move?

I am looking at
my big challenge...

How persistent am I
in pursuing that?

What is distracting me?

Who can help me
to stay focused on
what is important?

"Is it worth it to
surrender a grudge?
You can't hurt the perpetrator
by not forgiving,
but you can set yourself free
by forgiving."
~ Martin Seligman

How is forgiveness a
challenge for me?

What is in my best interest
moving forward?

Each action I take and
decision I make,
creates and
changes my future...

What is one easy step
I will take to move
in the direction
I wish to go?

I will ask these questions to
break those old habits that
keep me stuck in
the same old ruts.

1. How can I handle this
situation in a way *opposite*
from how I usually do?

2. Who inspires me?
How would they tackle
this issue?

Sometimes, the real
challenge is to pull back
and not act;
a challenge of inaction.

Where is inaction
a challenge for me?

What am I willing to
say "yes" to?

"The human spirit lives on creativity and dies in conformity and routine."
~ Vilayat Inayat Khan

Where am I dying?

How can I stop talking about "it" and start doing?

We all need allies to sustain
our momentum...

How can I create or
strengthen my support
system?

If I get creative and think,
who can I invite in?

"Dare To Suck..."
~ Carole King

How can allowing myself to
look foolish or
make a mistake open up
new choices and options?

Where am I willing to
swing out there and
take that chance?

"In a time of drastic change
it is the learners
who inherit the future.
The learned usually find
themselves equipped to live in
a world that no longer exists."
~ Eric Hoffer

How does this apply to me?

What is my challenge?

I have the most fun
when_____.

How can I invite
more of that into my life?

What commitment
will I make to that?

Who will I share that with?

I picture an anchor
around my ankle.

In my life,
who or what is that anchor?

Does the anchor
hold me back or
center me?

What is my challenge?

I look around and within.

I listen and notice.

What do I want to create?

Write that down...

What commitment
is called for?

How do I need to start my day to get off on the right foot?

What can I do that makes the rest of the day line up better?

What do I gain?

What am I ready to commit to?

_____

_____.

I can choose my own mindset.

Today I am *not* going to

_____.

Today I am going to

_____.

How can I remind myself of this
during my day?

C

"You gain strength, courage and confidence by every experience in which you really stop to look fear in the face. You must do the thing you think you cannot do."
~ Eleanor Roosevelt

What thing have I convinced myself I cannot do?

What is one BIG step that would take me closer to that?

At the end of each day,
can I say to myself,
"Because I am on this planet,
the world is a better place?"

What is my challenge?

What am I willing to commit to?

What will that look like?

Where in my life
do I need to stretch?

What would that feel like?

What would that look like?

What is the challenge
I am willing to commit to?

Where in my life is my attitude
in danger of becoming a
self-fulfilling prophecy?

What do I need to change?

What is my challenge?

C

What do I do, over and over,
that keeps me stuck when
I really want to move
forward?

What is my challenge?

Who can I talk
with about this that has
new perspectives?

Fill in the blank with either happiness or success:

Is my definition of

_____

narrow and unattainable?

How can I loosen or widen it?

What would this create?

How?

My challenge is to win the war.

What battle am I
willing to lose?

Within what battle can there be
no room for negotiation?

What will I say "no" to?

I really need to state this
important intention out loud...
I intend to

_____.

What if I were to tell
ten people about this?

How would that serve me?

I gather my courage...
Who will I share this with?

To me,
nothing is more important than
_____and

_____

and_____.

How can I challenge myself
to honor that?

How and where do I need to
step into being
a role model or a leader?

What step am I willing to take?

What will that sound like?

When was the last time
I laughed?

How can I do more of that?

What is my challenge?

What do I need to stretch?

What could I do every day
that would help to strengthen
my relationships with others?

...at home?
...at work?

I am willing to commit to

_____

and

_____.

When I lie dying,
what will I wish
I had done more of?

Who will I wish
I had spent more time with?

With that in mind,
what is my challenge today?

To protect my energy and
my time,
what is it okay for me
to say or do?

What will that look like?

What will that feel like?

What will that sound like?

When will I do that?

C

"I would like to do this **but**…"

Every time I hear myself say
that "but",
I will replace it with an "and".

Instead, I will say:
"I would like to

_____

and _____."

What challenge
appears for me?

"Ask and you will receive."

What do I want to ask for?

Will I commit to writing that down and
reminding myself daily?

is for

EMBRACE
and
ENERGY

Beliefs About
Embrace and Energy

Embracing the mindset that more *is indeed possible* opens you up to see and receive all that is possible.

The energy of the embrace is about
the big picture,
and the universe of possibilities.

Consciously asking yourself,
"What do I want to embrace and allow in,
instead of bracing against?"
invites a more expansive perspective.

After completing the first 4 steps of GRACE,
we arrive here at E.
A new direction, feeling, perspective or
attitude may surface.
It can feel the way
a painter views a blank canvas,
a gardener rich soil,
a dancer great music or
a writer a blank page.

Asking yourself,
"What do I want my energy to flow toward?",
can consciously change the flow of that
energy toward what you desire.

There is the energy and attitude of
expansiveness that asks,
"Where to from here?"

A Metaphor for
Embrace and Energy

It's a beautiful, sunny, warm
summer day.
I have been dreaming about
lazy, long, luxurious days,
where the
flowers are bursting with blooms,
the bees buzz and the birds sing.
Days where life has an ease
and a flow.

Where am I ready to bloom?

I have a dream...
Imagine it...

How can my energy flow
toward that dream today?

I have so many more options
than I think I have...

List the sensible as well as
the outrageous...

What are 3
other possibilities?

_____

_____

_____

Our energy is precious...

What do I want
my energy to flow to?

"I dwell in possibility."
~ Emily Dickinson

How can this
be my motto today?

Today...

_____

_____

If I could sit in a tall tree and
look down upon my
entire life,
what would I see as being
possible?

What is emerging?

What choices can I make to
brighten my life and
those around me?

If I could have anything...

What do I want?

Imagine that
I have all that I need...

What can I do
that would provide
vitality and positive energy
to my relationships?

I stand up,
take a deep breath,
plant my feet apart,
throw my arms wide and
look up into or
envision the clear blue sky.

What do I want to embrace?

What wants to embrace me?

What needs to be
said to me that will
keep my energy flowing
in a positive direction?

I stand up now and...

What do I say?

What do I want to invite into
my life that will
put a twinkle in my eye?

Find that place inside of me
where my *aliveness* lives...
can I describe that?

What is possible in my life
from that place of strength?

I think of
my biggest challenge...

What would be possible if,
instead of bracing against it,
I embraced this
challenge?

"Every day brings a chance
for you to draw a breath,
kick off your shoes and
dance."

~ Oprah Winfrey

For me, today, what does
this look like?

Where do I want to
focus my energy right now?

What is the impact I desire?

Picture the horizon
on the ocean at sunrise
with all its infinite wonder,
mystery and beauty...

What new day do I want to
invite into my life?

I think about my day...

What new perspective do
I need to embrace?

What new perspective do
I want to embrace?

How can I put my arms
around that?

I feel something new is evolving within me...

What is it?

How can I support this?

What feeds
my vitality and energy?

Where in my body does my
vitality and energy reside?

What's possible with
more of that?

Who is an inspiration to me?

Imagine that person
appears and
holds out their hand to me...

What are they encouraging
me to embrace?

I picture myself at home,
when I hear a knock at the
door. When the door opens,
I welcome into my home lots
of possibilities.
It's as if I just
invited my life in for a visit.

What came through my
door?

What do I want to embrace?

"Imagining what you want as if it already exists, opens the door to allow it to happen."
~ Shakti Gawain

Imagine it...

What "Ta-Da!" did I imagine?

Who would I be if
I let the world know who I am
instead of
who I think I should be?

Sometimes I feel like I am
shrinking and playing small...

What is possible if
I play large?

"Live out of your imagination,
not your history."
~ Stephen R. Covey

What is alive in
my imagination?

What does that look like?

Where does it
want to take me?

Think of my big dream...

What colors do I see?

What is my next
small step towards it?

What is my next big step?

Where in my life am I
choosing something different
than I would have
five years ago?

Where do I want to focus
my energy
to get me where I want
to be in the next five years?

I have a dream...

How can my energy flow
toward that dream today?

Think of a
beautiful night sky
full of stars...

What do I wish for?

My head wants me to
embrace

_____.

My heart wants me to
embrace

_____.

My soul wants me to
embrace

_____.

277

I sit quietly now
and count to 30.

Now, I ask myself,

"What wisdom,
already available in my soul,
wants to be embraced?"

If not now, when?

Imagine a genie
just popped out of a bottle...
And now I have
all the resources needed...

What is possible?

How can I bring light
into my life?

Where do I wish to
aim that light?

"Cultivate your garden...
follow your own bent,
pursue your curiosity bravely,
express yourself,
make your own harmony."
~ Will Durant

How can I cultivate
my garden?

What gift am I ready to
unwrap, enjoy
and embrace?

Sometimes I
push things away or
brace against them...

What if I could
stop pushing,
open my arms
and let life happen?

What is possible?

Pretend the sky is the limit...

What's possible now?

I received a letter from
someone who
loves and admires me.
It reminds me of
my forgotten possibilities.

What does the letter say?

"Focus on what you
are moving toward rather
than what you are
leaving behind."
~ Alan Cohen

What do I wish
to move toward?

I stand up tall and
throw my arms open...
and shout
"Ta-Da!"

What am I
envisioning and
inviting into my life?

If I didn't know my age,
what would I be doing?

I have goals in my life...

Right now, I will pretend
they have all been attained...

How does that feel?

What is possible with this
new feeling of power
inside me?

What is the universe
ready to offer me?

What am I ready to receive?

There are parts of me that
I have outgrown.

What is wishing to emerge?

What will that look like?

"When we die and
go to heaven,
we may be asked,
'Why didn't you become
you?' "
~ Elie Wiesel

What is possible if
I really become ME?

If I focus my energy there...
it will grow.

What do I want to expand
in my life?

I put my hand
over my heart and
say out loud,

"I lovingly accept myself
exactly as I am."

Take a breath...

What is possible from here?

The end...

How is it
really the beginning?

<u>Others are using</u>
<u>"Rise and Shine Anytime" to:</u>

- be more productive and creative
- connect with another person
- get unstuck
- clear mental clutter
- connect with intuition
- center themselves before or during an intense or adverse situation
- journal
- view life or current situation with the big picture in mind
- structure a group discussion {coaches, therapists, ministers, teachers, mentors, families...}
- cope with difficult life challenges
- clarify emotions
- enhance exercise {use while hiking, yoga, biking...}
- step into the present at work and home

Use this book while you *do* your life and experience the amazing results...

What Others Are Saying About
"Rise and Shine Anytime"

"This is a wonderful book that continues to bring new insight and answers after using it all these years. I highly recommend it to anyone who wishes to move forward with clarity and purpose in this fast paced world. It has changed our life."
~ Jon R. Jolles, MD

"I use "Rise and Shine Anytime" to clear the brain clutter and do a 360 degree view of my life. I can decide from there where to put my focus and emphasis and choose my next step."
~ Tracy Mindess, Life Coach

"I really like this book. It is very thought provoking. I find it helpful in my family especially with my parenting skills. I highly recommend this book."
~ Thomas Johnston, MD

"I eagerly recommend that others give "Rise and Shine Anytime" a chance. Now, whenever I find myself in a trying situation, I short circuit the anxiety by practicing the "G" in GRACE... Rather than jumping in and feeding the tense situation, I can let it pass while I think of the small miracles that have touched me."
~ Glenn Fratto, Chief Financial Officer

"I love this book. "Rise and Shine Anytime" gets me to see other possibilities and try things I would not have thought of previously. I can focus my energy and be more productive during stressful times at work. I keep a copy in my desk."
~ Erin Maness, Hospitality Industry

"This book is a positive life tool that is so neatly packaged into do-able quick-steps... I like it so much I bought one for each of my daughters. I know they will benefit as much as I have from all the wisdom in this little book. Thank you so much!"
~ Judy Kaplan, Parent

About the Author

Anne Barry Jolles is a Certified Life Coach, Author and National Speaker.

In addition to her 3 books and a CD, Anne presents workshops, retreats, tele-classes and seminars designed to deepen the learning and experience the energy of *"Rise and Shine Anytime"*. Her presentations are interactive, energizing, educational and tailored to suit the group's need.

Anne is a coach who supports a mix of personal and business clients who are committed to increasing life satisfaction, creating success, and obtaining a great quality of life and relationships at home, work and play.

Anne loves discovery. Her adventures include jumping off the "Jaws" bridge {"The shark's in the pond!"}, horseback riding through glacial fields with her family, and kayaking. She is an avid in-line skater and keeps her 'blades in her car trunk, just in case...

It has taken Anne 52 years to make the best chicken soup on the planet, and endless ballroom dance lessons to finally stop trying to lead and actually enjoy following.

Contact:
Anne Barry Jolles
781-878-8589
abjcoach@comcast.net
www.annejolles.com
www.riseandshineanytime.com

Other Titles by Anne Barry Jolles:

"G.R.A.C.E."
5 Steps For Bringing Your Best To The
Next Moment

"Keeping Your Sanity
While Loving and
Letting Go of Your Teen"
with a CD of same name.

"G.R.A.C.E."
for parents of teens
5 Steps for Bringing Your Best to the
Next Moment

All are available at www.annejolles.com
abjcoach@comcast.net
781.878.8589

A Gift For You!

6 Week Complimentary E-Course:
"Rise and Shine Anytime"

To sign up and receive this gift,
go to this website now:

www.riseandshineanytime.com

Wake Up Your Life!
- deepen your learning
- reinforce a new habit
- reminder of the concepts
- focus on what matters most

and
periodically receive inspiration,
updates, and new offerings
from Anne Jolles